The 8 Steps to Manifestation

The 8 Steps to Manifestation

A Handbook/Workbook for Conscious Creation

BIANCA GUERRA

LIVING LIFE PUBLISHING CO.

San Antonio, Texas
Sausalito, California

You may order directly from the publisher.

For information about permission to
reproduce excerpts from this book write to:

Living Life Publishing Co.
24165 IH-10 West, Suite 217-474
San Antonio, Texas 78257
Phone: 210-698-6392 • Fax: 210-698-6394
OR
1001 Bridgeway Blvd., Suite 704
Sausalito, California 94965
Phone: 415-331-9222 • Fax: 415-789-5834
OR
E-mail: LivingLifePublishing@msn.com
www.LivingLifePublishing.com

Library of Congress Control Number
2005903647
ISBN 0-9768773-9-2
Printed in China by Palace Press International
First Edition

The publisher commissioned Garret Moore to create the cover image entitled *8 Steps*.

All other images are © Digital Vision/Getty Images Pictures, Brand X/Getty Images Pictures, Photodisc/Getty Images Pictures, or Comstock/Getty Images Pictures.

Graphic Designer: Diane Rigoli
Editor: Judy Gitenstein
Editorial Consultant: Cynthia Rubin

Dedication

I dedicate this companion book to *A Woman's Guide to Manifestation* to all my friends who have been my support, my sounding board, and my palette on which I've been able to paint my life's story and from which I've learned my greatest lessons. To them I give my heartfelt love and acknowledgment for the role they have played in my life. I haven't walked this journey alone, as I've weaved in and out of the lives of so many. Each and every one of you has played an integral role in my development and life experiences and for this I give you my deepest thanks.

A special recognition and thanks goes to my parents, who are no longer with me, yet who gave me life and the stability and nurturance required for my tender development. I miss you both deeply.

To my loving and loyal sister, Sylvia, by whose example I've learned so much, I say thank you for being in my life and loving me unconditionally.

I also want to thank my two very best childhood friends, Jeanine and DeAnna, for the love, guidance, and support that they have given me throughout my life. Jeanine is with me still on this journey, always available, always supportive, and ready to be by my side at a moment's notice. Although DeAnna no longer walks this earth, I feel her loving presence in my life. I often reflect on her words of wisdom and keep them close to my heart. From her I learned my greatest lesson of humility and surrendering to the Divine will of God. With intense strength and faith in her Divinity she discovered her *true* essence and found her purpose in life. May we all be so blessed as to find our life's purpose.

To Mimi, Sera, and Peggy, and to the "Saddle Pal Gals," thank you, thank you, thank you, and thank you. You have unselfishly given me your love and support, guidance and friendship. You hold a special place in my heart and I want to acknowledge all of you for your ability to walk your talk and for embodying the meaning of what it is to be a true friend.

My love to all,
Bianca

Table of Contents

Preface

*T*his book is intended to carry the reader further and deeper to understanding and implementing the 8 steps to manifestation, as outlined in *A Woman's Guide to Manifestation: Creating Your Reality with Conscious Intent*. It is written with the sole purpose of creating a guide that will lead to the conscious manifestation of wonderful things.

Often you may think or feel or believe that you know what you want in life and know how to achieve or acquire it, yet are amazed as to why it doesn't happen. You may even have become complacent with the thought that you really didn't want it in the first place. This may make you feel a little better, yet doesn't help manifest what it is you REALLY want to create.

Understanding and incorporating the 8 steps to manifestation into your life is a marvelous tool to have in your toolbox. The 8 steps to manifestation can be used in every area of your life, whether it is to acquire more abundance, more joy, a better job, a wonderful relationship, or a healthy body and lifestyle, or just to create diversity and change. The 8 steps to manifestation offer a simple and effective way to achieve what you want in life. This easy-to-understand and easy-to-follow guide will lead you on a journey toward new and phenomenal discoveries. Included are worksheets to help you with this process and to make this book truly yours.

All is possible in the realm of possibilities. Welcome to this new world of possibilities and discoveries. If you can think it and imagine it, then you are more likely to create it, if you learn how to implement the 8 basic steps to manifestation. Be the co-creator of your world and enjoy and relish the fruits of your labor. Manifestation can be fulfilling and fun. Be aware and consciously choose what you want to manifest within your life. Apply these 8 easy steps to manifestation and allow them to assist you on your magnificent journey.

Be well, be safe, and be happy.

A Review of Manifestation and Your Role in Consciously Creating Goals and Desires

One of the key elements of fruitful manifestation is **knowing what you truly want to create.** Being awake and conscious of your place in life and knowing where you want to be is one important factor that assists you in manifesting your goals and heart's desires. If you are consciously aware of what you want, you increase the chances that you will get exactly that. If there is lack of awareness or direction in what you want to create or where you want to go, then what you manifest could be a complete and unpleasant surprise. You don't have to be fully conscious to manifest, yet realize that the end result of your creation may be something you hadn't originally bargained for.

Let's say you walk into a car dealership wanting to buy a new car. You are overcome with the amount of information from the salesperson and number of car models to choose from, not to mention color and accessories. If you weren't totally clear about what you wanted and needed in a vehicle nor had you really decided how much money you wanted to invest in this new purchase, you could end up leaving the car dealership with a car that is not well-suited to you and you could end up having severe "buyer's remorse."

If you are able to get in touch with your thoughts, feelings, and desires, then you are more likely to manifest what it is you want from life. Don't live life with your eyes shut or in denial. Be willing to see all aspects of your life. Tune into your inner guidance, your God-self, your Divinity, and find out where you need to be in life and what it is you want to create. The calm, centered, and peaceful knowing of what to do or what to create is generally a good indication for you that you have tapped into your inner knowing. Follow your intuition, your inner guidance, and begin the implementation of your manifestation. Learn to trust yourself and your intuition, your "gut feelings." Know that you have within you all the answers to all the questions you have or will ever have in life. Reflect on all the times you experienced a sense of inner knowing, a strong gut feeling that something was going to happen, and then it did. Use this example as a reference point to help teach yourself to trust your inner knowing. Know that this inner knowing, your inner Divinity, is never wrong. Embrace the courage to follow this inner guidance.

Conscious manifestation brings many rewards and with it many responsibilities. If you choose to live consciously, then you also choose to be responsible for your decisions, your actions, and your life. You then cannot place blame on anyone or anything outside yourself.

Know that with the responsibility also comes your power. In being responsible for your life, know that you are also the co-creator of it. You are the one creating all the scenes. Know you can have your life any way you choose. Don't let your responsibilities drag you down. Look at them as your ticket to taking charge of your life and manifesting your heart's desires. Be your own boss and learn to manifest the way you want.

So, if this is true, then whatever you have created, consciously or not, you can change or un-create. This can also apply to disease. Once you are conscious of your role in the

You Can Make a Difference

creation of your health (wellness and/or illness), know that you are powerful enough to change or reverse your state of health. If you have emphysema, and if you choose the course of prescribed therapy you feel is right for you and then choose to quit smoking and lead a healthier life, the chances are good that you will live a longer and more productive life. The same goes for eating healthy and exercising to maintain a healthy heart. Conscious knowledge, with the proper tools and commitment to a healthy life will, more often than not, give you that healthy life.

You have innate gifts with which you were born. You have also developed many gifts and talents along the way. Know that your gifts are unique to you and that with them you also carry your innate power. You have much to contribute to this world. There are many who have been positively affected by you and your uniqueness. Know that only you have experienced life in your shoes and those shoes are unique to you. Embody these gifts, talents, and qualities and know that in sharing them, they are multiplied. You have the power in your hands.

Be responsible and wise and choose to share with others. Open the door to your life and give someone that smile of love and acceptance or the helping hand of compassion and understanding. There is someone out there in this world who has been or will be influenced by you. Acknowledge this and commit to sharing more of yourself, you gifts and talents, with others less fortunate. Blessings not only go out to others, they also come back to you.

With conscious intent and with the help of the Divine, you can become the co-creator of your life. The supernatural help that you receive from a force greater than you, God is essential to actualizing your dreams and manifesting your heart's desire. Having the assistance of the Divine within you is such a simple yet VERY powerful ally in manifesting your desires. This power crosses the boundaries of mundane, earthbound laws. It steps into the realm of Spirit, of God, of the supernatural. With such great forces aligned with you and your purpose, you have increased your power and ability to manifest your heart's desires.

As an example, let's take the case of Edgar Cayce, the renowned medium/healer. He prevented his premature death when he chose not to step into an elevator occupied by other individuals. He sensed and/or noticed that the souls of the others in the elevator were no longer in their bodies. This was his supernatural message urging him not to enter the elevator, as something dangerous was probably going to happen. He was correct in his assumption: the elevator went down and crashed onto the bottom floor. Everyone in it perished. His co-creator, God, his inner Divinity, assisted him in choosing to stay out of the elevator, thus saving his life. All of you have access to this same assistance from God and your inner Divinity. Acknowledge its existence and tap into your resources.

You carry both masculine and feminine qualities within you. Knowing what each role represents and how it is played out in your life assists you greatly in achieving the life you want. The feminine role is the passive role, yet it is the role of the giver of life, of the receiver of blessings and abundance. This feminine side is also asked to ground the blessings received and then to nurture and share these blessings with her male counterpart. Conversely, the masculine side has the active role, the role of the giver of blessings and abundance. He is the provider and protector of his family and is the procurer of gifts. He allows the female to ground his gifts, to be nurtured by these gifts, and to then be led back to the Divine. Together both roles have a purpose, separately and united.

You move from one role to the other, regardless of your sex. Doing is action-oriented and considered a masculine quality while receiving is passive and considered a feminine quality. Sometimes you may be in the passive, yet creative, energy of the feminine that gives life. At other times, you may find yourself in the role of the male who is the provider and protector of the family, actively doing. This is not to say that one is better or greater than the other, only that one may be more appropriate in different circumstances. When you are in a relationship, it is often advantageous to assume the role given to you at birth. This is not to negate free will or free choice, only to say that if you assume the role that is innately yours, life usually moves more freely and the universal flow allows for greater, easier, and more effortless manifestation.

If what you want in life is to be a conscious creator or manifester, then assuming the feminine quality of receptivity will assist you in this task. Open yourself and your heart to receive the blessings from others and the Divine. The more open your heart is, the more love, blessings, and abundance can come into your life. Allow yourself to be open and vulnerable, and to receive. Know that in this opened vulnerability you also encounter your power. The power is derived from the ability to receive the multiple blessings given. The more you are able to receive, the greater the ability to manifest what you want. This makes you very powerful. You do not have to be a female to be good with creating or manifesting. The posture of being open and receptive, like an opened hand facing upward, or like a punch bowl right-side-up, is key to your ability to receive and hold the object/s and/or ingredients of your creation. You need to be the keeper of your dreams and to be able to hold them in a safe place until they come to fruition. Be the feminine/receptive and then follow the receipt of your gifts with a thank-you.

Manifesting relationships, in whatever form you want, is another aspect of utilizing your manifesting tools and skills. How you relate to others, whether it is in a parent-child or romantic relationship, or whether it is as sibling, friend, co-worker, or stranger, says much about how you relate to yourself

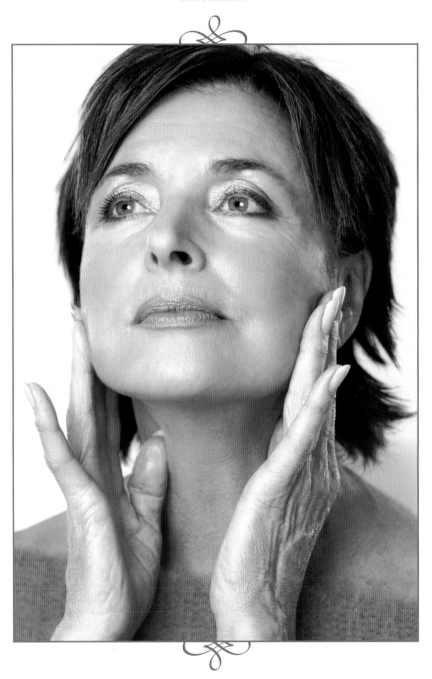

Be Your Own Best Friend

and to God, the Divine. How you treat yourself is generally an indication of how you treat others, whether you do so consciously or not.

Be conscious and responsible within your relationships with others. You can have the relationship of your dreams. In my case, my suppressed and very hidden anger manifested in my choosing men with angry and explosive tempers. My inability to recognize or express my hidden anger left me often feeling hurt and unloved following one of these reactive, angry responses from my mates. Look into yourself and see where you may be suppressing an emotion or living out someone else's drama. Don't allow yourself to be controlled by something you choose to avoid or deny.

Manifestation can be demonstrated in multiple forms. By this I mean that if you are not totally conscious about your life and what you want to create, you may be subconsciously or unconsciously creating your reality. Even stating something in a negative context can set the process of negative manifestation into motion. Having unconsciously set the scene and asking God to help me "break" from any limitations that I possible had, to experience life fully, actually led me down a path of learning how to function in life with a broken ankle. The injury occurred exactly eight days after that proclamation. So, I say, be careful with what you think and say, as you may be unconsciously setting a scene to manifest something into your life that you would not consciously want.

There is a fine line between manifestation and manipulation. I would like you to get a clear understanding between the two. Manifestation usually involves you and/or the cooperation or consent of another party. Everyone has chosen the object or situation to manifest, with a free will. Manipulation, conversely, takes away your free will. Someone else chooses the path, whether knowingly or unknowingly, whether by coercion or force. To manifest through manipulation carries a very high price tag and may result in a negative backlash. Universally, this goes against the flow and someone, somewhere, sometime will have to pay the price.

Manifest responsibly and ethically and allow others to experience their own manifestations. Don't decide what someone else is going to do or say or experience. Leave others to make their choices independently of your desires. Often you will encounter rebellion and frustration when you attempt to force your will onto someone or something else. Allow others to make their own mistakes and offer your love and gentle guidance instead. All will be better off when you do.

No one forces you to do what you don't want to do. If you find yourself living life in a way that isn't to your liking, know that on some level, conscious or not, you've made it happen, or allowed it to happen. If what you are feeling is the urge not to do something, then it is your responsibility to say no. Do not put the responsibility or blame onto others because you choose to be nice or polite or likable, when you really don't feel like it, or have said yes when you wanted to say no. Honor yourself and your feelings and allow yourself the freedom to speak what it is you truly feel. Do not fear rejection to your "no" response. Others will accept it and adapt. Know that the only one who truly suffers from your lack of ability to speak your true feelings is you. Be your own best friend. Stand up and support yourself the next time you are given the choice to say yes or no. You will be giving yourself the gift of empowerment.

When you've lost control of your life you've also lost control over your choices. Being out of control and locked in some other form of thought or emotion limits your ability to manifest what you truly want. Fear, pain, hurt, or anger is emotion that can take away your power to manifest consciously.

If you are being controlled by fear, you cannot make wise, conscious decisions about what you feel is your reality. This brings you out of choice and gives you possibilities based on fear. The result usually is some form of negativity or manifestation that you don't really want or didn't consciously ask for. Be centered and aware while enhancing your ability to manifest. If you are afraid to leave home and start a new life (i.e., leaving to go to college or moving to another city to start a new job), chances are high that you will not go or will fail in your new life or be miserable the entire time you are away from home. The fear of the unknown is very strong and a common theme among many, yet know that you will tend to attract what it is you fear the most. The more you focus on the object or situation that inspires fear, the greater the chance of it occurring.

Choose to live in love. Trust that all will turn out well and much better than you could ever imagine. Don't allow the element of fear to control you or your decisions. Experience the peacefulness of love and the inner knowing that you will be fine and are protected. Know that you are never alone.

Communication is essential for manifesting. It is also essential in the relationship with yourself and others. As the cells of your body depend on its innate ability to communicate, so does your life depend on your ability to communicate your wishes and desires to yourself, others, and God. Take the time to learn the languages of those with whom you choose to associate and learn the universal language of love. This form of communication will open many doors and will definitely assist you with the task of conscious manifestation. The better you are able to communicate your message to God and the Universe, the more quickly and easily your desires will manifest.

Being aware of consequence and able to live a life that you proclaim as yours is knowing how to walk your talk. You may feel you live in a manner that you believe to be true and authentic, yet life and people may mirror back to you something quite different. Be courageous enough to look at yourself honestly and

Observe What the World Mirrors to You

evaluate exactly what it is you proclaim as your truth. Ask yourself whether you truly live by your beliefs and convictions or are they just words spoken. Do you know what you believe and speak as your truth? If not, make an effort to dig deep within yourself and be willing to see the truth of what really is. Unless you admit to seeing and experiencing what truly is, you cannot change it for the better.

Be strong and courageous and choose to walk your talk. If one person tells you that you look and act like a camel, don't put much focus on it. If two people tell you that you look and act like a camel, you'd better start evaluating whether you are demonstrating these traits. If 20 or more people tell you that you look and act like a camel, chances are quite high that you probably ARE a camel. Be willing to see yourself honestly, not only through your eyes but also through the eyes of others you love.

No man is an island, so don't pretend you are alone. As stated earlier, learning to work and communicate within your community assists you on your path of conscious manifestation. Allow others to help you manifest, when appropriate, and accept the fact that you are not here on this planet alone. Learn to live and work in harmony with others and see how this magnifies your abilities to manifest your heart's desires. When your cells live in harmony with each other, health follows. So too does your life operate with the universal flow. Unify and work in harmony with yourself, others, and God. Reap the benefits of this beautiful union. Everyone has needed or will need the assistance of someone or something during his or her life. It's not selfish or weak to ask for assistance. Ask and you shall receive, yet know that the key here is to ASK.

Interacting within life usually generates beautiful and positive results and can assist you with manifesting your heart's desire, by contrast, reacting to people or situations is usually an unconscious and animalistic type of behavior and carries with it much negativity. You can definitely manifest during reactive moments, yet it usually is not what you would consciously choose to create. Drama is often intertwined within the reactive response and adds increased negativity to the equation while allowing for wasting of precious energy. Be conscious and responsible with your responses. Learn to give yourself some space and time to consciously choose an appropriate response. Don't allow yourself to fall victim to your primitive self. Be awake and aware and allow for conscious response. Think of the scenario of the two male dogs sniffing each other, then, in a reflexive movement, beginning to snarl and fight. Don't follow their lead. Use conscious choice, make responsible decisions, and choose to interact with others, rather than go into a reactive attack mode. So much hurt and violence could be prevented if only conscious interaction were the outlet instead of reflexive reaction. Don't be like the unconscious dog. Be the loving individual that you know you can be.

Living your life with an open heart, filled with love, greatly increases your ability to manifest. The manifestation you develop generally is filled with plentiful blessings. Love generates more love. The more love you give and receive, the more your heart can open. This is definitely a strong asset to have when manifesting your heart's desires. This is also a strong indication that what you choose to manifest will bring love and light to you and others. Be powerful and brave and choose to live life with an open heart.

Accept what "is" in life. If you are able to accept and tolerate what is, then you increase your ability to manifest more of the same or to change it to something more beneficial. If you live in denial or reject aspects of yourself or your life, then you become powerless to do anything about it. Don't simply reject what is not palatable to you. Recognize what is reality and then consciously choose what it is you want to create or change. You cannot change what it is you don't accept or acknowledge.

Be patient with yourself and others and learn that everyone is different. Learning to accept others for who and what they are allows you the freedom to do the same for yourself. If you do not admit that you have a problem with drinking, drugs, or cigarettes, then how can you consciously change it? How can you change something that you do not admit even exists? You can't. Don't fool yourself. You are the one you are truly hurting. Be real and be aware of consequence in your life and know what it is like to live with the freedom of the real you.

The shadow self is that aspect of you that lives in the dark, uneducated and uninformed, and that lives without love. Fear and love cannot exist within the same space, so if you love your shadow rather than fear it, you increase your chances of transforming your shadow self into a loving and more productive aspect of yourself.

Recognize fear for what it is. Everyone has experienced fear in some form or other during his or her lifetime. Fear should not be denied or negated. It should be recognized for what it is, a lack of love and light. Knowing this, one can be educated and guided back into the light. Once you are "in" love and "out of" fear, you greatly increase your ability to manifest your heart's desires. Don't hide in the shadow of your fear, as the fear will only multiply.

Understand that many people possess something within that may be considered a little frightening or scary, such as an explosive temper. If this sounds like you, don't let it get swallowed up in the dark shadows of your life. Let the air and the sunshine in to help you wash it away or transform it. Truly escaping from your inner fear is almost impossible; it goes where you go. Love it, understand it, and educate it into the light. Use the power of transformation to help create your heart's desires, not to hold something at bay. You will notice that your life will feel lighter and less worrisome while you feel stronger.

Transform Your Shadow Self

There should be a distinction between what may seem quite obvious: pleasure and pain. Pleasure is something that brings you joyful gratification and pain is a negative irritant of some sort. Often, a temporary pleasurable gratification carries with it a high price tag of pain, for example, a hangover following a night of drunkenness, or to divorce following an episode of infidelity. Pleasure-seeking is often destructive and hurts many in the process, mainly you. Be conscious and aware of what it is you really want to create and then decide just how important the temporary pleasure is. Weigh your choices and decide to choose wisely.

Anything is possible in the realm of possibilities, so why not reach for the stars? If you can visualize it, then more often than not you can consciously create it. Nothing limits you more than a lack of imagination and creativity. Be strong and choose the sweet life. Be willing to receive the many blessings this world and God have to give you. Be real and authentic and allow others to be who they truly are. Be at peace, accepting of yourself and the world. Learn what you came here to accomplish. Commit to your path and open your heart to receive the love, help, and guidance needed for your journey. Know that you are not alone.

Follow Your
Inner Guidance

One

Step 1 to Manifestation: Desire

"Desire. All creation begins with a desire for something.
The more energy infused into the desire and the more
your heart is involved in this process, the stronger the
force will be to assist you with your manifestation.
So, begin with a heartfelt emotion, a burning desire."

— from *A Woman's Guide to Manifestation*

Wanting or desiring something usually is the first step to bringing it into existence. The more you desire, the more likely you are to attain the object of your desire. If you don't want something "enough" you will not take the appropriate steps or put forth the required energy to get it.

Sometimes you may be very conscious of why you want something and other times you may just have a deep inner sense or emotional desire for something. Intellectually you may not quite know why you want it, yet the desire for it is there. It could be a word spoken that triggers your desire for something; it could be a simple glance, or something much deeper. It could be a burning desire that propels you to thought and action, a desire that keeps your attention most of your waking moments.

Here's an example: You dream of becoming a ballet dancer and you can see yourself doing just that. Your body, mind, emotion, and spirit are consumed with the desire to become a ballet dancer. You cannot see yourself doing anything else with your life. This, in my opinion, would be a burning desire to become or achieve something.

On the other hand, it could be just a simple word about food that could trigger your salivary glands to produce saliva and your olfactory glands to imagine a delicious smell, creating a desire to eat. A glance at a stylish outfit in a department store window may trigger you to want to buy it. Knowing that you will get some sort of pleasurable reward can also be a reason for desiring something. These are also examples of how you could be triggered to desire something, albeit something not very profound.

In your desire for something special, I hope for you that the object of your desire is something that is good and healthy and will be of some benefit, yet this does not have to be a precursor to desire. You can desire something totally inappropriate and unhealthy, such as someone else's spouse or job. You may desire drugs or alcohol or that extra piece of chocolate cake.

Whatever it is that you desire, know that the mere fact you "desire" something puts the acquisition into motion. Be aware and conscious of what it is you really want, to help facilitate its occurrence. Be clear with yourself as to what you want so this desire can then be transferred into the Universe to begin the setup of your co-creation with God. The clearer the desire and intent, the greater cooperation you will receive from God, the Universe, and those around you.

Eliciting help from others to attain what you desire is also a factor in its occurrence. If you can relay your intense desire to others so they can feel your burning passion, there is a greater chance that you will receive their help. People, the Universe, and

God are available to help those who are ready to help them-selves. If you can indicate that you are truly desirous of some-thing, you will likely attain it with the assistance from others, if that is your intent.

Isn't it easier to teach someone who is eager to learn, or to work with someone who is always available with assistance? So too will the Universe, God, and individuals be fired up to help you if you indicate your burning desire to achieve and/or acquire something. Know that you do not have to achieve alone. There are generally others who think and feel as you do who would be more than willing to assist you to gain or achieve what you desire.

"Desire" worksheet

1. List your innermost desires in order of preference.

"Desire" worksheet

2. List when and how often you focus on each of your desires.

"Desire" worksheet

3. List the reason(s) that you feel you desire a certain thing or scenario.

"Desire" worksheet

4. Describe what it feels like to live with or have attained your desire(s).

"Desire" worksheet

5. Describe what it looks like to live with or have attained your desire(s).

"Desire" worksheet

6. Define what it sounds like to live with or have achieved your desire(s).

"Desire" worksheet

7. Describe what it smells like to live with or have achieved your desire(s).

"Desire" worksheet

8. Describe what it tastes like to live with or have achieved
   your desire(s).

"Desire" worksheet

9. Write a brief story about each of your desires and how they would be of benefit in your life.

Visualize Your
Heart's Desire

– Two –

Step 2 to Manifestation: Thought

*"Thought. Desire is then transferred into the mental body,
where you begin thinking of ways to create/manifest what
you want. The more you focus on how you are to manifest
your desire, the likelier you will be to create it. If you can
visualize what you want to manifest and can see yourself
getting it, this will add power to your manifestation.
Focusing your thoughts and images like a laser beam is a
strong and powerful tool to assist with your manifestation."*

— from *A Woman's Guide to Manifestation*

*T*hinking about what you want is your second step to manifestation. Once you have identified the burning desire of
what you want to have or create, you can then begin the
conscious, intellectual process of thought, of dreaming of your
desire. As you think, dream, plan, and visualize yourself having
or creating what you desire, you begin the process of energet-
ically creating the blueprint of what it is you want. Like an
architect who draws the blueprint of the building he or she is
going to build, so too do you draw your own set of blueprints
for your creation.

The clearer you make the blueprints, the greater and more intense your focus, the more exact your creation will be. Walking yourself through the blueprints, the way an architect does, checking all angles, pathways, materials, and dimensions, will give you a much better sense of what it is you are creating and whether you really want it a certain way. Taking yourself through possible scenarios and creating different sets of blueprints enhances the likelihood of your getting exactly what you want.

Imagine yourself creating a virtual reality of your future, placing yourself in the middle of this reality and, for just a moment, living out your dream, your desire. What does the experience feel like? Are you happy? By creating this virtual reality you are giving yourself a glimpse of what life would be like with the object of your desire. You will know a little better whether you really want to live this way or not.

Create for yourself multiple scenarios for your future and choose the one that best suits your life and needs. My experience in life has been this: If I can visualize myself a certain way or in a particular situation, then that's been my license to create it. If, on the other hand, I've had difficulties seeing or feeling myself in a certain scenario, then I've had great difficulties creating it or things didn't quite turn out the way I had intended.

So, I say, if you can see it, visualize it, feel it, and sense it, then you are on your way to creating it. The more physical senses incorporated into the virtual reality of your life, the greater the chance you have of bringing it in into actual reality.

You may begin with your visualization by feeling that it's really just a game—just pretend—and that nothing will come of it, yet be aware that the brain doesn't know the difference. As discussed in A Woman's Guide to Manifestation the brain doesn't know whether you are dreaming about running or actually running. It will release, within the body, the appropriate responses associated with running (i.e., elevated heart rate and increased perspiration).

So, if in doubt, trust that God, the Universe, and your internal wisdom knows what to do, and you then can follow these directives in creating your heart's desires.

"Thought" worksheet

1. Write a step-by-step plan for how to manifest your desire(s). Create your own blueprint of your new life.

"Thought" worksheet

2. Write a second plan, or blueprint, for how to manifest your desire(s).

"Thought" worksheet

3. Write a third and completely different plan for how to
   manifest your desire(s).

"Thought" worksheet

4. List the choices for your future that you have before you.

"Thought" worksheet

5. List the changes in your future life that you can see.

"Thought" worksheet

6. List the future life changes that you like.

"Thought" worksheet

7. List the future life changes that you do not like.

"Thought" worksheet

8. While visualizing your new life, list the people you are with and the locations you are in.

"Thought" worksheet

9. Create a virtual reality of your new life with your desire(s). Be specific and utilize your five senses during the experience. Describe the experience in detail.

Ask for Divine Guidance

Three

Step 3 to Manifestation: Verbal Proclamation

"Verbal proclamation. Speaking your thoughts and desires out loud begins setting the manifestation in motion. You can either state what it is you want or ask God and the Universe to assist you in manifesting what you want. In speaking out loud, you are demonstrating to the Universe, to the world, to your friends and family that you are going to manifest your desires. The more you speak the words with conviction, as if what they describe has already occurred, the likelier it will be that they will manifest."

— from *A Woman's Guide to Manifestation*

Words are powerful, so much so that a single word can create miracles. A single word can also destroy. Let's take for example the words "go" and "stop." They both are single-syllable words that denote strong messages. When you hear "go," you body might react with an openness and eagerness to move forward and perform the task at hand. "Go" is an empowering word. You generally carry with you a feeling of being supported and encouraged to complete the task. You may feel a sense of limitless possibilities and a hope that all will turn out well and in your favor.

When you hear the word "stop," your body might react in a completely different way. The mechanisms in your body will generally apply the brakes, on all levels, and forward motion will cease. For a split second, you may find yourself suspended without thought or action, not knowing what to expect next. The word "stop" carries with it a sense of fear or danger. Feelings of limitless possibilities are generally stunted and you may even feel somewhat paralyzed.

All these feelings, thoughts, and emotions generally occur simultaneously and often as reflexes. When you are conditioned to react to certain words in certain ways, it often happens without thought. If you bring conscious awareness into your words and your proclamations you will soon discover that you will create more opportunities in life to your liking. If you add to your conscious awareness the assistance from God, the Universe, your Divinity, by the mere fact of your asking, you will increase the possibilities of creating what you want, and in record time.

You can create both good and not-so-good results with your spoken words. It's so much better to be conscious of what comes out of your mouth so that you can create wonderful things in your life. Negative and harmful words are just as powerful and likely to be instruments of your creation as are positive and loving words. By staying conscious and in your heart you will increase the likelihood of creating or manifesting your heart's desires.

Ask and you shall receive. This is so true for me and I would love for you to experience this phenomenon as well. By asking God and the Universe, and by incorporating the assistance of your inner Divinity, you are increasing the avenues by which you can create or manifest your heart's desires. Speak the words out loud and allow them to be created in physical form. Speak your desires out loud, allow them to reverberate within your world and the Universe, and see how much faster the physical form will manifest.

You are the initiator, the instigator, of your reality. Be aware and conscious and make responsible decisions as to what you truly want from life, in your life, and then go for it. Nothing can stop your progress more than you. Set your sights to "go" and allow yourself to proclaim what your want for yourself. It is possible for you to have what you want. You are the one who holds the key.

"Verbal Proclamation" worksheet

1. Write down, with clarity, what you want to proclaim to God and the Universe. Speak these words out loud.

"Verbal Proclamation" worksheet

2. Write down, and then say out loud, what you want to say to your friends and family. Be clear and specific about what you want them to hear.

"Verbal Proclamation" worksheet

3. Know what you want to manifest and write down the specifics of what you need assistance with.

"Verbal Proclamation" worksheet

4. Know what you want to manifest and write down the specific group of people you intend to ask for help.

"Verbal Proclamation" worksheet

5. Listen to yourself proclaim out loud your desires of what you
   want to manifest and write down the responses you receive
   from others.

"Verbal Proclamation" worksheet

6. Write down the thoughts that surface following your verbal proclamations.

"Verbal Proclamation" worksheet

7. Write down the feelings you experience following your verbal proclamations.

"Verbal Proclamation" worksheet

8. Write down the changes in your life that you've noticed following your verbal proclamations.

"Verbal Proclamation" worksheet

9. Visualize yourself in your new life, and then describe a scenario in which you express your thoughts, words, and feelings. Include the thoughts, words, and feelings of those close to you.

You Deserve the Best

– Four –

Step 4 to Manifestation: Belief

*"Belief. Knowing 100 percent, like an innocent child,
that you will succeed in creating your heart's desires is
essential for your manifestation. Believe, without question
or doubt, that you will create and manifest what it is
you've proclaimed to God and the Universe.
Believe that you deserve the results of your creation."*

— from *A Woman's Guide to Manifestation*

To believe and to know that what you want can be yours, 100 percent, is your fourth step to manifesting your dreams and heart's desires. If you know and believe that you will pass a test, the likelihood of your doing so is high. If your feel healthy and believe, at a very deep level, that you are healthy, chances are great that you are healthy. If there is no doubt in your mind that you will succeed at a certain task, you will, more often than not, succeed.

Let's take for example a child who knows, 100 percent, that he or she does not like a certain food. It's almost impossible to change the child's opinion as to his or her likes and dislikes and even more difficult to force that child to eat something that he or she doesn't want. Somewhere, deep inside the mind of that child, he or she knows and believes that the unpleasant-tasting food will not be eaten and there is not much you can do about it other than forcing the child to swallow, and not spit up (a very difficult task).

You can also create your reality if you believe, 100 percent, like an innocent child, that you will get what you want and that you deserve to get your heart's desires. An innocent child usually does not question his or her ability or right to receive. He or she only knows and believes that desire, turned into thought, verbally proclaimed (via shouting, crying, or demanding), usually results in getting/receiving.

Why not develop this inner knowing, this confidence and strong sense of self as seen in children? Begin utilizing these characteristics in your co-creation with God, your inner Divinity. Leave doubt by the wayside and focus all your energies on attaining what you desire. Try not to second-guess yourself or predict the outcome of your wanting something. Simply be witness to the wonderful and beautiful scenarios you create.

If you leave no room for doubt to enter your plan and use all your energy with focused intent to manifest your heart's desires, you are more than likely going to achieve your goal. Even one percent of doubt can sabotage your plans. Why chance limiting your progress and success?

Trust yourself, God, and the Universe and allow yourself to know and believe that life can be the way you want to create it. Test your abilities to manifest and see the result of your creation. If you believe and know that something is true, it is true for you. Keeping this in mind is vital to creating what you want the way you want it. Having a desire with a plan to implement it, along with your verbal proclamation to the world, is the foundation to getting what you want. Believing and knowing it will happen will be an important catalyst that will make it happen.

"Belief" worksheet

1. Make a list of what you believe 100 percent you can manifest.

"Belief" worksheet

2. Describe your understanding of manifestation.

"Belief" worksheet

3. Enumerate any doubts you may have about your manifestation of your desire(s).

"Belief" worksheet

4. List the reason(s) why you believe you deserve to receive the manifestation of your desire(s).

"Belief" worksheet

5. Describe your feelings about yourself.

"Belief" worksheet

6. What are your most outstanding qualities?

"Belief" worksheet

7. List your most trustworthy qualities.

"Belief" worksheet

8. Describe how you view the world.

"Belief" worksheet

9. Describe how you would live your life if miracles really occurred.

Live in Harmony with Your Feminine Receptive

– Five –

Step 5 to Manifestation: Receiving

*"Receiving. Receiving is an integral part of the process
of manifesting. Open your heart and drop into your
feminine/receptive mode, and allow yourself to receive
the wonderful gifts of your creation. By being in your
feminine/receptive mode, you allow yourself to receive the
object of your desires. By "feminine/receptive," I'm not
implying you have to be a female to manifest, only that you
must embody this feminine quality of receptivity."*

— from A WOMAN'S GUIDE TO MANIFESTATION

*T*o receive is a feminine, passive quality. I'm not saying that
you do nothing when receiving. You are the cup/chalice
that needs to be present to receive the energy, the wisdom, and
the object of your desires. Your cup needs to be strong enough
to hold these qualities.

Much power and responsibility is associated with the feminine, passive, receptive cup/chalice. Without it, there is no form.
All falls on empty ground. The feminine/receptive quality is not
the active doer; it embodies the quality of passive being-ness. The
cup/chalice just is. It exists. It doesn't have to do anything other

than receive. The stronger the cup/chalice, the more it can receive and hold, and thus the more your cup allows you to create.

All of us have the feminine/receptive cup/chalice within. It's the recognizing or failing to recognize its existence that is often the key factor in our success with manifestation. If you don't understand your role as the receiver to your creative desires, then you aren't able to capitalize on your gifts. As you accumulate your desires, blueprints, virtual realities, where do you think they end up? Yes, your cup/chalice. It's your container, your safe womb. They stay in this container/womb until you're ready to give birth to the idea, to the desire.

Men can give birth and do so on a regular basis, as in the birth of a nation, the birth of an idea, the birth of a business. It's your feminine/receptive creative element that comes into play during manifestation. We all have the same qualities. It's just that not all of us are fully aware of our feminine power. Through the feminine comes life in all forms. Know this as your truth and implement this aspect into your formula to help create your reality.

Embrace your feminine/receptive quality. Don't fight or negate it. It is the power and vessel needed to incubate your desires and to help bring them into physical form. It is not a weak quality, but is soft and often heartfelt. Open your heart to love and to experience the gentle, soft quality of your cup/chalice and you will know its strength and stability. Without it, you will have great difficulties creating your reality, your heart's desires.

Intuition is another element of the feminine/receptive and is an avenue that allows you to receive important information that is often required in knowing what step to take next. Learn to trust this innate quality you possess and utilize it for your highest good. Honor your feminine quality and help develop it to further serve you and others.

"Receiving" worksheet

1. Describe what the feminine/receptive means for you.

"Receiving" worksheet

2. Describe what being the cup/chalice means for you.

"Receiving" worksheet

3. List the times you have felt that you have embodied the feminine/receptive role.

"Receiving" worksheet

4. List what happens for you when you are in the feminine/
   receptive role.

"Receiving" worksheet

5. What are your opinions on the strengths of the feminine/
   receptive quality?

"Receiving" worksheet

6. What are your opinions on the weaknesses of the feminine/receptive quality?

"Receiving" worksheet

7. List occasions you have given birth to new and creative ideas.

"Receiving" worksheet

8. List situations where you've successfully used your feminine
   intuition.

"Receiving" worksheet

9. Write a short story about your life from the perspective of a feminine/receptive individual, while imagining there are no limits to your creative potential.

Support Yourself

Six

Step 6 to Manifestation: Grounding into the Physical

"Grounding into the physical. Once you receive the object of your desires, you can then integrate it and ground it into the feminine earth for its physical manifestation. By grounding, I mean that you take the energy of your desire, claim it as yours, and allow the physical form to take shape. The more you connect with Mother Earth and her feminine principles of creation and birth, the likelier you will be to manifest your desires."

— from *A Woman's Guide to Manifestation*

Grounding yourself into the physical is very similar to the roots of a tree. The deeper and thicker the root system, the bigger and taller the tree can grow. The size of the tree is often proportional to the size, depth, and strength of the root system. Other factors, such as the wind and physical resistance of other kinds, can also make an impact on the root system and the integrity of the tree.

So too does your personal root system have a strong impact on the growth of your desire. The deeper and stronger your roots are planted, the likelier the desire of your creation will grow into fruition. The stronger and more firmly grounded your foundation, the greater the chance your creation will stand the test of time and become a permanent acquisition.

By this I mean that you need clarity of desire, detailed blueprints of your desire with an experience of a virtual reality, and the physical sense, of how your life would be once your desire were actualized. Verbal proclamation of your desires made to God, the Universe, family, and friends with a deep inner belief that you will manifest your desires also helps. Open your heart to receive the new life while not being afraid of the change. Be open to give and receive the love that will come with your new life.

The more you implement these steps, and the more strongly you can see, hear, smell, taste, and touch these desires as realities, the more likely you will create them. Dig into the ground and plant your seeds with the extended root system and watch the tree grow up into your world of reality. Without pre-planning and planting what you want and how you want it, you may not quite get what you desire.

Do the groundwork required to harvest your crop. It's very basic and simple, yet it does require time and a commitment to see the process to the end. Be the one who reaps the benefits of your labor and flourish in your accomplishments. You are the creator, the planter of your life, so you are also the one who can then manifest your heart's desires. Be your strong and resilient, feminine/receptive root system and watch in awe at shaping your life's creation just the way you want it. Know that you can create your life any way you want if you are conscious and clear about what you want and follow the appropriate steps in its creation.

Be the roots of your own tree and give yourself the stability and opportunity to grow as tall and as wide as you want. Allow yourself to manifest your heart's desire with all the help and support your roots can supply.

"Grounding" worksheet

1. Describe the root system of your life.

"Grounding" worksheet

2. Where are you planted and where do your roots go?

"Grounding" worksheet

3. Describe what type of tree you view yourself as and why.

"Grounding" worksheet

4. Describe what seeds you desire to plant for your future.

"Grounding" worksheet

5. Elaborate on how you plan to nurture these seeds of desire to fruition.

"Grounding" worksheet

6. Describe the tools and individuals you will require to reap the harvest of your manifestation.

"Grounding" worksheet

7. Describe your life, as you imagine it, with the fruits of your labor.

"Grounding" worksheet

8. List those individuals who will be with you to share in your harvest.

"Grounding" worksheet

9. Write a short story about your life from the confines of the earth that holds your seeds and nourishes the root system for the creation of your heart's desire(s).

Know that Help
is On the Way

– Seven –

Step 7 to Manifestation: Letting Go

"Letting go. Allowing God and the Universe to take over and orchestrate the how, when, where, and why of your creation is vital to its manifestation. The harder you struggle for control over universal law, the more difficult it will be to manifest your desires. You've done your part by setting the intent. Allow God and the Universe to determine the particulars. Allow the process to occur in Divine time. If you do so, you will find that the results of your manifestation are far greater and more beautiful than what you had originally imagined."

— from *A WOMAN'S GUIDE TO MANIFESTATION*

There are certain things that are under your control and other things that are not. One of the things that you do have control over is desiring what you want and setting the ball into motion to create or manifest it. The previous six steps have been laid out for you to mull over and incorporate into your life. Once you have completed the first six steps to manifestation, let go of the outcome and allow God and the Universe to take over.

Just as you cannot control the growth rate of a tree, so too is it difficult to control the rate of your manifestation. Of course there are guidelines you can follow, but in the end, the only force that controls this Universe is God. Allow God to help with your creation and rest assured that you will receive this help. Like ingredients coming together to create a delicious cake, so too can your heart's desire become a reality.

Let go of what happens in the oven while your cake is baking and just know that the result will be phenomenal. Most probably it will turn out far better than if you worried and constantly opened the oven door to check on how it is doing. Trust in yourself and your decisions to co-create your heart's desires with God, the Universe, and your Divinity. You could not have better partners in your corner.

Imagine yourself in a relationship where there is a lot of push and pull. When you pull in one direction, your partner pulls in the opposite direction. Then suddenly you choose to stop pulling. What happens next? Your partner loses momentum and falls backward because there is no counterforce. What I'm trying to say is that all the pushing in the world isn't going to make your cake, or your heart's desires, more appealing or manifest faster. It only wastes your time and energy, which could be used for more interesting and rewarding tasks. You could be nurturing yourself and/or others or you could be initiating the manifestation of a new heart's desire. There is no law that says you have to wait until one desire is actualized to begin pursuing another. Your possibilities are limitless. You alone decide what you want to create and when to set the ball in motion for its creation.

Trust that your creation is undergoing its proper incubation period and that all will manifest in its Divine time. You've done your part and now it's time to relax and let go. Allow your seeds to gestate for proper growth and development and be the witness to what blossoms.

"Letting Go" worksheet

1. Express your feelings on what letting go means to you.

"Letting Go" worksheet

2. Express any concerns you may have about letting go.

"Letting Go" worksheet

3. Describe the difference, as you understand it, between letting go and giving up.

"Letting Go" worksheet

4. Describe a situation you were in where you had no option but to let go.

"Letting Go" worksheet

5. Describe the worse scenario that could happen if you were to surrender and let go.

"Letting Go" worksheet

6. Describe the best scenario that could happen if you were to surrender and let go.

"Letting Go" worksheet

7. Describe what it would take for you to trust God and the Universe to support you in letting go.

"Letting Go" worksheet

8. Describe what your life would look like if you did not have any worries about your future.

"Letting Go" worksheet

9. Describe how you could help others learn how to surrender and let go.

Give Thanks

– Eight –

Step 8 to Manifestation: Gratitude

"Gratitude. Giving thanks to God, the Universal Intelligence, is one of the steps that help to self-perpetuate manifestation. By acknowledging that you have received help from some other level that you have tapped into-Divinity-you are stating that it is done. It is like saying 'Amen.' You are giving finality to your manifestation and setting up the cycle for more manifestation down the road."

— from *A WOMAN'S GUIDE TO MANIFESTATION*

Giving thanks and being grateful for the manifestation of your heart's desires is a very simple, very powerful thing to do. When you open your heart and genuinely offer gratitude to that force greater than you and to your inner Divinity, you are honoring the wonderful blessings you have just received through manifestation. This in turn allows the self-perpetuation of the creation of your heart's desires.

Voicing gratitude, with authenticity, teaches you and others that you are not alone and did not create your desires alone. You always have your Divine force and that of God and the Universe with you. All you need to do is acknowledge that there is a force and power greater than you that is ready and willing to help.

Isn't it more enjoyable to continue giving when the person whom you've given to is grateful and honors your giving? Somehow, this gratitude elicits the desire to give more. I know that I tend to give more, and with greater affection, to those who don't expect it and to others who show genuine gratitude. It's only natural. Like attracts like. The more you give and feel you are giving to the right person or cause, the more you want to give, especially if the recipient indicates that he or she is appreciative of your help.

Would you still be able to actualize your heart's desires without showing gratitude? Possibly yes, although you may be limiting yourself with the amount and degree of manifesting. You would not be setting up a cycle for self-perpetuating more of the same creation. Ingratitude doesn't get you too far. Why not open your possibilities to create more and even greater manifestations of your desires?

Be your own well of gratitude for yourself and others. Live life with appreciation for what you have, what you have created, and what you are still to create. Know that the more you understand and appreciate that your life and everything in it is a gift from a higher power, the easier it will be for you to give gratitude to God and the Higher Intelligence within you. Living your life in grace and with gratitude is one way to embody your power of manifestation fully. Fill yourself with gratefulness for living and for the life you've created for yourself and know that your life is in your power. Use your power wisely. Don't abuse this power but be grateful that it exists within you.

"Gratitude" worksheet

1. Make a list of those to whom you are grateful.

"Gratitude" worksheet

2. List what you are grateful for.

"Gratitude" worksheet

3. Describe your idea of what genuine gratitude is.

"Gratitude" worksheet

4. List the individuals who have shown you gratitude.

"Gratitude" worksheet

5. List the occasions you have expressed gratitude.

"Gratitude" worksheet

6. Express what it feels like to receive gratitude.

"Gratitude" worksheet

7. Express what it feels like to give gratitude.

"Gratitude" worksheet

8. Describe the methods you would use in assisting others to understand and express gratitude.

"Gratitude" worksheet

9. Write a short account of your future utilizing gratitude as your theme.

You Create Your Reality

– Nine –

In Summary

*H*ere is a review of the 8 Steps to Manifestation. What follows is a visualization and affirmation to use whenever you like, every time you want to manifest something in your life.

Desire:

    A. Have a desire: the more passionate and intense, the better.

    B. Have clarity with what you desire and follow your inner guidance.

    C. Allow yourself to exude your desire(s) and to express it/ them to God, to the Universe, and to others.

Thought:

    A. Once you've clarified one of your heart's desires, begin with your visualizations on how you plan to create it.

    B. Draw multiple blueprints of your new life and incorporate your heart's desire within it.

    C. Mentally focus on your new life while creating a virtual reality utilizing your five senses.

Verbal Proclamation:

    A. Know that your words are very powerful.

    B. Have clarity with and be conscious of what it is you want to verbally declare for yourself.

    C. Ask for Divine guidance and help and you will receive it.

Belief:

A. Incorporate a 100 percent belief and knowledge that you will have what you are planning on manifesting.

B. Trust your knowing and allow this knowing to guide your steps.

C. Feel that you deserve to receive the very best life has to offer.

Receiving:

A. Embrace your feminine/receptive quality of passive strength.

B. Become the cup/chalice that holds the object(s) of your desire for creation.

C. Give birth to your desires by opening up to your feminine/receptive side and learn to share these gifts.

Grounding into the Physical:

A. Dig deep within your feminine earth quality and plant the seeds of your desired manifestation.

B. Become the strong roots to your developing tree and learn to support yourself.

C. Commit to doing the work required for your desire(s) to take root.

Letting Go:

A. Once you have walked through the previous six steps to create your manifestation, learn to let go of any attachment to the outcome.

B. Know that your cake will bake and be complete in its proper and Divine time.

C. Trust in God and the Universe and know that help is on the way.

Gratitude:

A. Giving thanks with genuine gratitude will generate more of the same.

B. Be your own wellspring of gratitude and learn to live in thanks and grace.

C. Your life is a gift. Learn to appreciate it and be grateful.

Visualization/Affirmation

I imagine myself living a life that no longer holds much meaning. I search deeply within myself and notice a burning **desire** to change my life, as I know it. The more I focus within, the more I notice that this **desire** is growing, and all I can focus on, during my waking moments, is this inner **desire** for change.

I then begin with **thoughts** on how I can create this change within my life. I **think** of multiple scenarios on what my new life will look like. My **thoughts** travel over what I will look like in my new life. My **thoughts** also cover my new career, new relationship, and new home. I can smell my surroundings and can almost taste the pastries my neighborhood bakery is preparing. I can even hear what my neighbors and co-workers are saying and notice that they are even talking about me. My **thoughts** take me into a virtual reality where I can feel what it would be like in my new world. It feels good and I definitely can imagine myself living this new life in my **thoughts**.

I then make a decision to change my life and begin **verbally proclaiming** to my family, friends, co-workers, and immediate boss that I want to change my life and career. The more I outwardly **speak** about what I want to do, the more I realize that people begin to **believe** me, and the more I realize that I really want to do it. I then realize that **speaking** about wanting to change has shifted into my actually making the change.

Now that I made my career change, have moved into a new home, and have begun a new life, my deep **belief** that I will be happy is instrumental to my success. I have no doubt that I've chosen the right path. I have this inner **knowledge** and excitement that my life is right on track. My trust and **belief** in my chosen path is as strong and innocent as a child **believing** that he or she will be fed when hungry. I have no worries. I know and **believe** that my new life is just what I need to embody and experience.

Once I am living my new life, I realize that to facilitate the completion of my **desired** change, I need to open myself to **receive** the blessings from God, from the Universe, from my environment, and from myself. Becoming my **feminine/receptive** allows me to be the cup/chalice that holds my **desired** result in a safe, gestational environment. I know that in proper Divine time, I will manifest the finished product of my new life. Keeping my **desired** life in the **feminine/receptive** womb allows me to live and experience my life without fear of destroying my hopes and dreams. I intuitively **know** that I will be fine in my new chosen world and that, in time, I will actually see and experience what it is I already know to be true. I've chosen the path that is right for me.

Becoming **grounded** and planting myself deep within the earth to allow myself to be **rooted** in my new life takes time and patience. A tree doesn't grow overnight. I **know** that with proper care and nurturance, my planted tree will take root and form the strong foundation for the growth of my tree, my new life. I allow my tree, my new life, to grow at its own pace, making sure that I stay **grounded** in the **knowledge** that I have chosen wisely. Life takes on new meaning; I am witness to my role as co-creator of my new life.

Once I've finished the task of completing the first six steps to manifestation, I realize now that I can **let go**, rest, and allow my new life to unfold. This is the most pleasant part of my journey as I watch my life transform into a more beautiful and productive one. By **letting go** of when and how it is all to happen, I've discovered the secret to its manifestation. I've learned that by allowing God and the Universe to take over, my life is so much more blissful than I could have imagined.

In this blissful state of being, I automatically feel the need to **give thanks** and **gratitude** to God and the world at large for allowing me this opportunity to experience this life of my own creation. What power and what joy I experience in the **knowing** that my life is in my own hands and that I can have what I want if I know how to utilize the proper tools to create it, and for this **knowing** and experience, I am so **grateful**.

May peace and blessings accompany me on this journey through life.

About the Author

BIANCA GUERRA is the founder and owner of Bianca Productions LLC, a multimedia production company that develops conscious content for broadcast radio and television, DVD, and broadband Internet distribution. She is also the founder and owner of Living Life Publishing Co., a San Antonio, Texas- and Sausalito, California-based publishing company that develops and publishes book, cards, and electronic media dedicated to uplifting and educating its readers.

Ms. Guerra earned a Bachelor of Science in Physical Therapy and Biology from Texas Woman's University in Denton, Texas in 1974. She also studied energy medicine and the healing arts and graduated with honors as a Master Energy Healer. Along with being a self-taught medical intuitive, Ms. Guerra has studied many additional forms of energy and spiritual healing, including homeopathy and Reiki. She was ordained as a hands-on healing minister in 1992 when she earned a Bachelor of Ministerial Science.

She sold her Physical Therapy and Sports Medicine practice in 1990 to pursue additional education in holistic and alternative medicine. She is committed to helping the individual consciously awaken by helping to connect with his or her inner wisdom.

She is a member of the American Physical Therapy Association (APTA), and the National Association of Television

Program Executives (NAPTE), a life member and diplomate of The American Association of Integrative Medicine (AAIM), and a Life Fellow Member and Advisory Board Member of the American College of Wellness (ACW).

Ms. Guerra divides her time between San Antonio, Texas, and Sausalito, California.

Please visit her websites at:
www.BiancaProductions.com
&
www.LivingLifePublishing.com.

Other Titles by Bianca Guerra

A Woman's Guide to Manifestation:
Creating Your Reality with Conscious Intent
A 240-page book detailing how you can become
the master creator of your life.
Price: $19.95 hardcover
ISBN: 0-9768773-0-9
Or $15.95 paperback
ISBN: 0-9768773-1-7

A Woman's Guide to Manifestation
The inspirational cards created from the book:
a 44-card deck with a 64-page instructional booklet.
Price: $15.95, ISBN: 0-9768773-3-3

InnerScope™
Self-Awareness Cards
A 44-card deck with a 40-page instructional booklet.
Price: $15.95, ISBN: 0-9768773-4-1

Other Titles offered by
Bianca Productions LLC and
Living Life Publishing Co.

SuperLove
By Lou CasaBianca
A beautifully designed and illustrated book
depicting the journey and experience of sacred love.

SuperLove Cards
By Lou CasaBianca
A Companion to the book "SuperLove"
A 44 Card Deck with instructional booklet.

For more information about the author and/or how to order,
please visit our website at:
www.LivingLifePublishing.com

Living Life
Publishing Co.

About Bianca Productions LLC
dba: Living Live Publishing Co.

Purpose

The purpose of our business, Bianca Productions LLC (BPLLC) dba: Living Life Publishing Co. (LLPC), is to help enlighten individuals through education while enriching them through awareness of their innate abilities to create their own reality. BPLLC and LLPC incorporate the premise that everyone has the ability to heal him or herself and his or her life if only awakened to this inner wisdom.

It is through the medium of radio, television, audiovisuals, and published written materials that this company will focus on helping to bring alternative health, healing, knowledge, abundance, and consciousness into the mainstream.

Mission Statement

"The mission of Living Life Publishing Co. is to help enlighten, enrich, and empower the lives of others via the avenue of multimedia. Our goal is to help bring an individual into a heightened sense of awareness of his or her strengths and life's purpose. Living Life Publishing Co. strives to promote a more socially conscious and responsible person who can contribute to positive changes in the world."

—Bianca Guerra, October 2004